Travel Guide To Guimarães 2023

Discovering Guimaraes: A Journey Through Portugal's Historic Gem

Timothy S. Govea

Copyright © 2023 Timothy S. Govea

All rights reserved. No part of this book may be reproduced, stored in a retrieval system, or transmitted in any form or by any means, electronic, mechanical, photocopying, recording, or otherwise, without the prior written permission of the publisher.

Table Of Contents

INTRODUCTION

Welcome to Guimaraes: A Snapshot of Portugal's Historic Gem

GETTING TO KNOW GUIMARAES

The History and Heritage of Guimaraes

Geography and Climate: When to Visit

Practical Travel Information: Visa, Currency and Language

TOP ATTRACTIONS IN GUIMARAES

Guimaraes Castle: The Heart of the City

Palace of the Dukes of Braganza: A Royal Residence

Nossa Senhora da Oliveira Church: An Architectural Marvel

Alberto Sampaio Museum: Art and Culture in Guimarães

EXPLORING GUIMARAES' NEIGHBOURHOODS

- Santiago District: The Old Town's Enchanting Charm
- Oliveira do Castelo: Where History And Modernity Meet
- Creixomil: Embracing Nature And Tranquility

IMMERSING IN GUIMARAES' CULTURE

- Festivals and Events: Celebrations Not to Miss
- Gastronomy and Culinary Delights: Must-Try Dishes and Restaurants
- Traditional Crafts: Shopping for Local Artisanal Products

OUTDOOR ADVENTURES IN GUIMARAES

DAY TRIPS FROM GUIMARAES

- Braga: A Pilgrimage to Portugal's

Religious Capital

Amarante: A Riverside Escape

Douro Valley: Wine Tasting Amidst Vineyard

PRACTICAL TIPS FOR A SMOOTH TRIP

Transportation Options: Getting Around Guimaraes

Accommodations: Where to Stay for Every Budget

Safety and Health: Staying Well-informed

Additional Resources and Websites

LANGUAGE AND USEFUL PHRASES

Basic Portuguese Expressions for Travelers

GUIMARAES TRAVEL ITINERARIES

One-Day Explorations

Weekend Getaways

Extended Stay Adventures

CONCLUSION
Final Thoughts

INTRODUCTION

Welcome to Guimaraes: A Snapshot of Portugal's Historic Gem

Guimaraes, a town in Portugal's gorgeous north, is a living example of the nation's rich history and cultural legacy. This picturesque city, frequently referred to as the "Cradle of Portugal," has a particular place in the hearts of its residents and the country at large.

You will be taken back in time to the beginnings of Portugal's nationhood as soon as you set foot in the ancient cobblestone alleyways, where tales converge with reality and history whispers its secrets.

An Overview of Guimaraes's Prodigious Past

- The history of Guimaraes extends back to before Portugal became a sovereign nation. Folklore holds that Countess

Mumadona Dias founded a convent here in the ninth century to defend the local populace against the Moors. Her deeds created the groundwork for Guimaraes, and later for the entire nation.

Afonso Henriques, the first King of Portugal, was born in Guimaraes in the 12th century and started the process of gaining the nation's independence. It is hardly surprising that the city has achieved the prestigious status of UNESCO World Heritage site due to its historical significance.

Beautiful architecture and historic sites

- You will be in amazement as you travel through Guimaraes because of its beautiful architecture and preserved landmarks. The city's recognizable symbol, Guimaraes Castle, is proudly perched atop a hill and provides sweeping views of the area. With its massive stone walls and watchtowers, this mediaeval stronghold inspires awe and transports visitors to an era of knights and noble adventures.

- Another important sight, the Palace of the Dukes of Braganza, exhibits the splendour and opulence of Portuguese royalty. The palace provides a window into the opulent lifestyles of earlier kings with its elaborate Gothic and Renaissance architecture. It seems like entering a historical novel as you meander through its opulent rooms and meticulously maintained grounds.

Immersive Cultural Traditions & Experiences

- Guimaraes attracts tourists with rich cultural experiences and centuries-old traditions in addition to its architectural wonders. The city comes alive all year long with festivals and events that capture the lively energy of its residents.

From the Festival of Sao Gualter through the White Night, people from all over the world gather to celebrate the celebrations as the streets are decked out in vibrant decorations and music fills the air.

- The city's fabric is heavily woven with art and craftsmanship, and traditional crafts are still in high demand in marketplaces and workshops. The artists of Guimaraes proudly display their talents and convey their enthusiasm for protecting their cultural heritage via everything from beautiful pottery to delicate lacework.

Outdoor recreation and the beauty of nature

- In addition to being rich in history and culture, Guimaraes is also surrounded by stunning natural beauty. There are lots of chances for outdoor activities in the lush landscapes, rolling hills, and peaceful forests that surround the city.

  You'll be rewarded with breathtaking views of Guimaraes and the surrounding countryside if you take a stroll up Penha Mountain. Guimaraes City Park provides a tranquil place for outings and leisure where you may relax and get in touch with nature.

Conclusion

Guimaraes is a captivating city that gives visitors a greater understanding of Portugal's outstanding history and cultural heritage. Its protected landmarks, exciting festivals, and friendly people all combine to create an unforgettable experience that stays in visitors' minds long after they leave. Whatever your interests—history, culture, or nature—Guimaraes has something magical to offer and begs you to explore it to learn more about Portugal's historical treasure.

GETTING TO KNOW GUIMARAES

The History and Heritage of Guimaraes

Guimaraes' history and heritage are intricately entwined with Portugal's development as an independent country. This picturesque city has a special place in the history of the nation because it was crucial to the establishment of the Portuguese monarchy.

Early Foundation and Settlement:

- The history of Guimaraes began long ago when Celtic tribes lived in the area. Roman and Moorish influences could be seen throughout the ages, but it wasn't until the 9th century that the city's history truly changed. Legend has it that Countess Mumadona Dias, a noblewoman, built a monastery there to shield the locals from Muslim attacks. Guimaraes' development was made possible by this deed of generosity, and the monastery transformed into a settlement that the city grew up around.

Creating a Nation:

- The 12th century was the most significant period in Guimaraes' history. Around 1109, Afonso Henriques, the country's first monarch, was born in this city. Afonso Henriques led the struggle to free the County of Portugal from the Kingdom of Leon. He was a brave and visionary fighter.

- He gained possession of the County of Portugal in 1128 by defeating his mother, Countess Teresa of Leon, and her lover, Fernao Peres de Trava, at the Battle of Sao Mamede. After years of conflict with the Moors and other adversaries, Afonso Henriques crowned himself the first King of Portugal on July 25, 1139, establishing the nation's rule.

The Salado Battle and Guimaraes Castle:

- During the early years of the Portuguese kingdom, Guimaraes Castle, built atop a hill overlooking the city, was important. It acted as a tactical military stronghold, aiding in the consolidation of the newly constituted nation and providing protection from invasion.

- The Battle of Salado in 1340 is one of the major incidents in the castle's past. The invasion of the Castilian army, under the command of Alfonso XI, was successfully stopped by King Afonso IV of Portugal during this fight. The nascent kingdom was preserved thanks to Portugal's independence and sovereignty being firmly established after the Battle of Salado.

As the First Capital: Guimaraes

- The honour of being Portugal's first capital belongs to Guimaraes. Afonso Henriques picked Guimarães as his capital after ascending to the throne, and it held that position until Lisbon took it over in 1143.

  Guimaraes maintained its relevance and continued to flourish as a significant political, cultural, and commercial centre despite losing its position as the capital.

World Heritage Site of the UNESCO

- Guimaraes was named a UNESCO World Heritage site in 2001 in honour of its historical importance and admirably preserved mediaeval buildings. The historical district of the city exhibits its rich legacy and attracts tourists from all over the world with its winding streets, historic buildings, and particular charm.

Guimaraes still serves as a symbol of the tenacity and perseverance of the early Portuguese settlers who built the country's basis for unity and independence.

Travellers have a deeper understanding of the history and heritage that influenced modern Portugal as they experience its cobblestone streets, historic sites, and vibrant culture. The legacy of Guimaraes is still shining brilliantly and capturing the hearts of everyone who enters its storied embrace.

Geography and Climate: When to Visit

Guimaraes geography

- In the Minho region of northern Portugal, Guimaraes is situated. It is located around 55 kilometres (34 miles) northeast of Porto, which is the second-largest city in the nation.

  The city is picturesquely surrounded by greenery, rolling hills, and rich valleys, making it a popular vacation spot for those who enjoy the outdoors and the great outdoors.

- Guimaraes is traversed by the Ave River, which enhances the city's natural attractiveness and offers tourists a tranquil setting. Because of its advantageous location close to the Spanish border, Guimaraes has historically served as a crucial crossroads for trade and cultural interaction.

Guimarães' climate:

- Due to its location near the Atlantic Ocean, Guimaraes has a temperate marine climate. Because of its moderate winters and beautiful summers, the city is a lovely place to visit for most of the year.

When to Go to Guimaraes:

- The ideal time to travel to Guimaraes mostly relies on personal tastes and the kind of adventure tourists are looking for. Every season has its benefits, and the city's cultural calendar is constantly packed with events and festivals.

- **Spring (March to May)**: Guimaraes is a wonderful place to visit in the springtime. The temperature is beginning to rise, and the landscape is alive with vibrant blossoms. It's the perfect season for outdoor pursuits like hiking, park exploration, and gorgeous scenery enjoyment.

- **Summer (June to August)**: Summertime in Guimaraes means pleasant weather and longer daylight hours. There are several outdoor events, concerts, and street festivals, which give the city a lively feel. However, summer is also the busiest travel season, so be prepared for heavier people and more expensive lodging.

- **Autumn (September to November):** Guimaraes is beautiful in the autumn. As the temperatures steadily drop, ideal circumstances for sightseeing and outdoor activities are created. The city's beauty is enhanced by the fall foliage, which offers wonderful possibilities for scenic driving and photography.

- **Winter (December to February):** Guimaraes experiences a reasonably mild winter with sporadic showers and chilly temperatures. Visitors can enjoy touring the city's historical landmarks without the crowds even though they may not be as popular with tourists. The city keeps its beauty. During the holiday season, it's also a wonderful opportunity to indulge in substantial Portuguese cuisine and take part in local customs.

Unique Occasions and Festivals:

- Several notable occasions and festivals are held in Guimaraes throughout the year, which adds to the city's appeal as a tourism destination. Among the most well-known occasions to celebrate are:

- A vibrant historical reenactment was held in August to celebrate Saint Gualter, the city's patron saint. White Night is an all-night cultural festival in September that features music, art, and performances. Carnival is a vivid and colourful celebration that takes place in February or March and includes parades, costumes, and other events.

In summary, Guimaraes is a fascinating place that can be enjoyed all year long, with each season having its special appeal.

Guimaraes welcomes guests with open arms and a plethora of unforgettable cultural experiences, regardless of whether you prefer the busy energy of summer, the vibrant blooms of spring, the crisp air of autumn, or the quiet atmosphere of winter.

Practical Travel Information: Visa, Currency and Language

1. **Visa Requirements:** Portugal, including Guimaraes, abides by the Schengen visa regulations as a member of the Schengen Area of the European Union.

   Numerous nationalities can enter Portugal without a visa for brief stays (often up to 90 days within 180 days). However, depending on the traveller's nationality, different visas are needed.

2. Using their national ID cards, citizens of the European Union, the European Economic Area (EEA), and Switzerland can enter Portugal. Visas are not required for entry for citizens of nations that have visa-free agreements with the Schengen Area. However, nationals of non-exempt nations must apply for a Schengen visa at their home

nation's Portuguese consulate or embassy.

3. Travellers must make sure they are aware of their nationality's visa requirements and processing dates well in advance of their intended trip.

4. **Currency & Money Issues:** The Euro (EUR, €) is Portugal's official currency. Before landing in Guimaraes, it is important to exchange money, especially if you are flying into a smaller airport or are coming from a non-Eurozone nation. In bigger cities, you can also get currency exchange services at banks, exchange offices, and some hotels.

5. The majority of hotels, eateries, and shops in Guimaraes accept major credit and debit cards including Visa and MasterCard. To be safe, always

have extra cash on hand for smaller businesses, public transportation, and other scenarios where cards could not be accepted.

6. In Guimaraes, there are many ATMs (cash machines) where visitors can withdraw cash using their debit or credit cards. Keep in mind that potential ATM fees can change based on the card issuer and the ATM network being used.

7. Portuguese is the official language of Portugal. Although younger generations and tourists frequently speak English, particularly in major cities, you can run into people who speak the language poorly in more isolated or rural locations.

8. Basic Portuguese can be learned, and the locals will find it useful. When

making friends with the individuals you meet while travelling, a few simple greetings, thank yous and pleases can go a long way.

9. Language hurdles can be overcome and your travel experience improved by using phrasebooks or translation applications.

10. **Time zone:** Guimaraes lies in the Western European Time Zone (WET), which runs from the last Sunday in March to the last Sunday in October. WET is UTC+0 during standard time and UTC+1 during daylight saving time (WEST).

11. **Electricity**: Portugal's electrical system operates at 230V and 50Hz. The two-pin European Type C and Type F power connectors are the industry standard. To utilise their electrical

equipment, tourists from nations with various plug types will need a travel adaptor.

Emergency Contact Information: Dial these numbers in case of an emergency:

- Emergency medical services/ambulance: 112
- 112 Police
- Fire: 112

To guarantee a smooth and comfortable voyage to this fascinating location, it is advised to check for any updates or changes in travel laws, currency conversion rates, and other relevant practical information before setting off on your trip to Guimaraes.

TOP ATTRACTIONS IN GUIMARAES

Guimaraes Castle: The Heart of the City

Castle Guimaraes: The Center of the City

The beautiful protector and emblem of the city's illustrious past, Guimaraes Castle is perched haughtily on a hill covered in luxuriant greenery.

This mediaeval stronghold transports tourists back in time to the early years of Portugal's nationhood with its massive stone walls and soaring watchtowers.

Guimaraes Castle, one of the most important historical sites in the area, is beloved by both locals and visitors, perfectly encapsulating Portugal's rich cultural legacy.

A Fortress With History:

- The history of Guimaraes Castle, often called the Castle of Guimaraes, dates back to the tenth century. It was initially built as a fortress to defend the area from Moorish incursions.

  The castle experienced numerous additions and alterations over the years, each of which reflected the prevailing architectural trends.

Arrangement and Architecture:

- The layout of the castle is a superb illustration of mediaeval military construction. Its strategic towers, battlements, and thick stone walls demonstrate the genius of its architects in building a powerful stronghold. A large gatehouse with mediaeval accents and a drawbridge that originally guarded the entry greets tourists as they approach the castle.

- The Tower of the Homage (Torre de Menagem), which functioned as the castle's lords' house and was the fortress's centre, is one of the many areas that tourists can explore inside the castle's walls.

Visitors who ascend the tower's winding stairs are rewarded with spectacular panoramas of the surrounding city and countryside that give them a sense of the town's attractive and historic location.

Historical Relevance

- Afonso Henriques, the first King of Portugal, was born at Guimaraes Castle, which has enormous historical significance. According to legend, Afonso was born inside the castle walls in 1109, solidifying the castle's significance in the establishment of the Portuguese kingdom. Afonso Henriques started his campaign for independence from Guimaraes, which ultimately resulted in his coronation as king in 1139.

- The fortress' historical significance was further cemented by the Battle of Sao Mamede, fought close to the castle in 1128 and a turning point in the fight for independence.

UNESCO Recognition and Preservation:

- Guimaraes Castle endured periods of deterioration and abandonment over the years. However, attempts were made to protect and repair this national monument throughout the

20th century. It now functions as a living museum, an exceptional example of mediaeval military architecture, and enables visitors to travel back in time and get fully immersed in Portugal's intriguing history.

- In 2001, Guimaraes Castle and the town's historic core were recognized as UNESCO World Heritage sites in recognition of their cultural and historical importance. The castle will be preserved and protected thanks to this honourable designation so that future generations can enjoy it and learn from it.

Guimaraes Castle excursion:

- A journey through history takes place in Guimaraes Castle, giving tourists a chance to engage with the country's historical foundations. Information boards and guided tours offer insightful perspectives into the history of the castle and its significance in determining Portugal's future.

Guimaraes Castle is a must-see location for history buffs, lovers of architecture, and anybody looking to learn more about Portugal's cultural legacy. It invites visitors to enter the past and enjoy the rich tapestry of the country's history.

Palace of the Dukes of Braganza: A Royal Residence

Royal Residence: Palace of the Dukes of Braganza

The Palace of the Dukes of Braganza, located in the centre of Guimaraes, is a stunning reminder of Portugal's illustrious history. This majestic mansion provides tourists with a look into the affluent lifestyle of the Portuguese nobility through its extravagant architecture and regal charisma.

The palace, one of Guimaraes' most important historical sites, functions as a living museum, maintaining the opulence and rich cultural history of a bygone era.

Origins and History:

- The history of the Palace of the Dukes of Braganza spans several centuries.

The first Duke of Braganza, Dom Afonso, a notable nobleman and military commander, constructed it in the 15th century. The wealthy Braganza family, who were influential in Portugal's history and later assumed the position of monarch, lived in the palace as their home.

Architectural Glamour

- The palace's design, which combines Gothic and Renaissance elements, displays the wealth and taste of the Braganza family.

  While the interior features exquisitely designed ceilings, elaborate woodwork, and luxuriously equipped rooms, the façade is embellished with decorative windows, ornate carvings, and stone battlements.

Palace highlights include:

- The Palace of the Dukes of Braganza offers enthralling tours of its numerous rooms and halls, each of which has a distinct charm and historical value. The following are some noteworthy highlights:

- **The Chapel:** The Braganza family had a strong spiritual commitment, which is reflected in the chapel, a modest but splendid church inside the palace, decorated with stunning religious art and elaborate decoration.

- **The Great Hall**: The ducal court would meet in this vast hall to conduct major events and rituals because of its lofty ceilings and big windows.

- **The Duke's Room:** The lavish living quarters of the duke, furnished with priceless artwork and furniture, offer a glimpse into the rich lifestyle of the nobility.

- The Tapestry Room is a showcase of the palace's taste in luxury and artistic expression. It is adorned with gorgeous tapestries and elaborate embellishments.

Restoration and Preservation

- The Palace of the Dukes of Braganza experienced periods of neglect and deterioration over the centuries, like many other historical structures. However, major efforts were made in the 20th century to conserve and repair this architectural treasure.

The palace still stands as a revered monument today, allowing tourists to travel back in time and experience the beauty of Portugal's aristocratic past.

Going to the Palace:

- A journey through Portugal's royal past is provided by a visit to the Palace of the Dukes of Braganza. Guided tours and educational exhibits offer insightful perspectives into the Braganza family's lives and the palace's historic significance.

  The palace's surrounding grounds, which are exquisitely landscaped, add to the allure by encouraging guests to take strolls and soak in the tranquil atmosphere.

The Palace of the Dukes of Braganza in Guimaraes is a must-see location for history buffs, art connoisseurs, and anybody interested in Portugal's aristocratic past. It provides a window into the opulent world of the Portuguese nobles and the splendour of their royal house.

Nossa Senhora da Oliveira Church: An Architectural Marvel

The Nossa Senhora da Oliveira Church is a marvel of architecture.

The Nossa Senhora da Oliveira Church, located in the centre of Guimaraes, is a stunning architectural wonder that honours the city's extensive religious and cultural legacy. This church, one of the most revered religious monuments in the area, has won the hearts of both tourists and residents with its elegant exterior, detailed features, and historical significance.

Origins and History:

- Nossa Senhora da Oliveira Church's beginnings can be found in the 12th century, in the early years of Portugal's independence.

  According to legend, the church was constructed on the spot where Countess Mumadona Dias, the town's founder, had dedicated a shrine to the Virgin Mary, whom she thought had miraculously spared her from peril.

  The original shrine changed over time to become the magnificent church that exists today.

Architectural Glamour

- Nossa Senhora da Oliveira Church is a distinctive fusion of architectural styles that showcases the influences of several historical eras. Its facade, which demonstrates the development of architectural tastes over time, is a tasteful fusion of Romanesque, Gothic, and Manueline features.

- A Romanesque doorway with exquisite sculptures of biblical scenes and mythical animals serves as the church's principal entrance.

  A rose window over the door adds a touch of elegance and lets soft, filtered light into the room. The fine stonework and ornate decoration on the facade showcase the period's skilled artisans' work.

The Holy Sacrament Chapel

- The Holy Sacrament Chapel (Capela do Santissimo Sacramento) is one of Nossa Senhora da Oliveira Church's most notable features. This church, which was built during the Manueline era, is an exquisite illustration of the beautiful and complex Manueline style.

  The Manueline architectural style is evident throughout the chapel's interior decoration, which includes fine ribbed vaulting, delicate tracery, and nautical elements like twisted ropes and seashells.

The Legend of the Olive Tree

- Nossa Senhora da Oliveira (Our Lady of the Olive Tree), the name of the church, is based on a local myth. The church's courtyard previously had a hallowed olive tree there, according to mythology. According to legend, the olive tree appeared out of thin air when the first temple was constructed. For the residents of Guimaraes, the olive tree evolved into a representation of hope, serenity, and safety.

Relevance to Religion:

- Generations of believers have visited and worshipped at Nossa Senhora da Oliveira Church. The church is still a busy house of worship, holding regular Masses, religious festivities, and other events.

  The city's religious and cultural identity has continued to be strongly influenced by devotion to Our Lady of the Olive Tree.

Visiting the Church of Nossa Senhora da Oliveira:

- Nossa Senhora da Oliveira Church offers visitors to Guimaraes a chance to delve into the past while also taking in the complex beauty of the building's design.

    For anyone looking to gain a deeper understanding of Portugal's religious tradition and cultural legacy, the church is a must-visit location due to its serene atmosphere and historical significance.

Nossa Senhora da Oliveira Church invites you to be immersed in the timeless beauty and profound spirituality of this magnificent architectural gem in the centre of Guimaraes, whether you are an architecture enthusiast, a history lover, or a pilgrim seeking spiritual solace.

Alberto Sampaio Museum:Art and Culture in Guimarães

Guimarães' Alberto Sampaio Museum of Art and Culture

In Guimaraes, the Alberto Sampaio Museum is a shining example of art, history, and culture and provides an enthralling tour of the area's cultural legacy.

This museum, which is housed in a former monastery, features a substantial collection of religious artwork, historical relics, and cultural treasures that shed light on the city's past and its significance as a Portuguese cultural hub.

Location and History:

- Alberto Sampaio, a prominent Portuguese historian and academic who devoted his life to conserving and promoting his nation's cultural history, is honoured by having his name given to the museum. The Nossa Senhora da Oliveira Church and the well-known Guimaraes Castle are both close to the museum's central location in Guimaraes.

Given that the structure is a 14th-century architectural marvel, its location within the former Convent of Saint Dominic (Convento de So Domingos) lends a sense of historical continuity.

Collections and Displays

- The Alberto Sampaio Museum is home to a sizable and varied collection that covers several eras of Portuguese history. Numerous themed exhibitions that provide a window into the artistic, religious, and cultural features of

Guimaraes and the surrounding area are available for visitors to explore. Among the highlights are:

- **Religious Art:** The museum's collection of religious art includes a variety of complex altarpieces, sculptures, and antiques. These works of religious art offer insights into the area's intense religious activities and devotion to the divine.

- Textiles and embroidery: The museum has a wonderful collection of textiles and embroidery that displays the fine artistry and workmanship of regional craftspeople throughout history.

- Visitors can be in awe of a variety of expertly created metals, such as chalices, reliquaries, and sacred vessels, as well as exquisitely glazed ceramics that reflect the area's long standing artisanal traditions.

- **Domestic Life Artefacts**: The museum also has several domestic life artefacts, including furniture, ceramics, and household goods, which allow visitors to get a look into Guimaraes' residents' daily lives over the years.

- **Temporary Exhibitions:** In addition to its permanent holdings, the museum frequently presents temporary exhibitions of modern art, historical subjects, and cultural issues pertinent to Guimaraes and Portugal.

Education and Preservation

- The Alberto Sampaio Museum is actively involved in the preservation and study of the area's cultural legacy in addition to functioning as an exhibition space. The priceless works of art and historical relics are meticulously preserved through conservation efforts so that future generations can enjoy them.

- The museum also serves an important educational function by providing workshops, tours with guides, and educational activities for both kids and adults. These programs seek to increase knowledge of Guimaraes' historical significance while fostering a love for art and culture.

The Alberto Sampaio Museum visit:

The Alberto Sampaio Museum is a lovely cultural attraction that immerses tourists in the aesthetic and historical fabric of Guimaraes and the area around it. The museum offers a fascinating and educational experience that complements the city's other historical sites and deepens Guimaraes' alluring appeal, whether you are an art aficionado, a history buff, or simply interested in Portugal's rich cultural legacy.

EXPLORING GUIMARAES' NEIGHBOURHOODS

Santiago District: The Old Town's Enchanting Charm

Santiago District, which is tucked away in the centre of Guimaraes, has a classic charm that takes visitors back in time.

This alluring old town is a living witness to Guimaraes' rich cultural legacy and its significance as the home of Portugal's nationhood.

It is steeped in history and architectural magnificence. Walking through the Santiago District's winding cobblestone streets is like taking a trip through time, as each step reveals a different aspect of the city's storied past.

Historical Relevance

- Because Guimaraes played a significant part in the founding of Portugal within these ancient walls, Santiago District is important to the history of Portugal. The first King of Portugal, Afonso Henriques, was born in this region in the 12th century.

  The city's historical importance earned it the moniker "the cradle of Portugal," making it a popular destination for residents and visitors desiring to learn more about the country's origins.

Mediaeval Buildings:

- Beautiful specimens of mediaeval architecture fill the streets of Santiago District, each facade evoking personality and charm. A combination of Romanesque, Gothic, and

Renaissance architectural elements that reflect the passage of time and the city's ongoing history may be seen in the buildings' wonderfully maintained characteristics.

In addition to serving as evidence of Guimaraes' previous prosperity, the architecture mesmerises tourists with its intricate design and fine craftsmanship.

Castle Guimaraes:

- The renowned Guimaraes Castle, a magnificent fortification that serves as the city's emblem, is located in the centre of Santiago District. The castle's imposing walls and strong watchtowers provide commanding views of the surroundings, highlighting the location's strategic significance. A fascinating experience that immerses tourists in the turbulent past that shaped Guimaraes and Portugal as a whole is exploring the castle grounds.

Leandro de Oliveira

- Largo da Oliveira, a lively area in Santiago District, sits at the nexus of modernity and antiquity. Its name comes from the peace-and-prosperity-symbolising ancient olive tree that originally stood here.

  The Nossa Senhora da Oliveira Church is one of several old-fashioned stores, lovely cafes, and historical sites that line the area. It's a fun spot to enjoy the regional cuisine, observe people, and take in the vibrant atmosphere of Guimaraes' culture.

Church of Nossa Senhora da Oliveira:

- The Nossa Senhora da Oliveira Church, a spectacular religious structure that personifies the city's devotion to religion, is situated above Largo da Oliveira.

  A remarkable fusion of architectural styles, including Romanesque, Gothic, and Manueline influences, can be seen in the church's construction. Beautiful altarpieces and religious art decorate the inside, reflecting the city's long standing religious traditions.

Keeping Cultural Heritage Safe:

- The significance of Santiago District as a UNESCO World legacy site highlights how crucial it is to conserve cultural legacy for upcoming generations. The district's charming appeal will continue to amaze visitors for years to come because of the city's dedication to maintaining the historical integrity of the area.

Conclusion:

Santiago District in Guimaraes is a true gem because of its alluring attractiveness and historical significance. Visitors become a part of the living past that moulded Portugal's character as they wander the winding alleyways, take in the ancient architecture, and immerse themselves in the rich cultural heritage.

Travellers are encouraged by Santiago District's ageless allure to embrace the past, the present, and the spirit of a city that holds the secrets to Portugal's national identity and cultural legacy.

Oliveira do Castelo: Where History And Modernity Meet

Oliveira do Castelo: Where Modernity and History Collide

Oliveira do Castelo, which is located in the centre of Guimaraes, is a compelling neighbourhood that skillfully combines the energetic pulse of current life with the echoes of history.

This neighbourhood preserves its treasured historical landmarks while accepting current influences, acting as a living example of Guimaraes' progress.

Oliveira do Castelo is a wonderfully alluring location since it offers travellers a seamless fusion of the past and present as they stroll through its picturesque streets and discover its cultural treasures.

Historical Relevance

- The traces of Guimaraes' lengthy and illustrious past may be seen in Oliveira do Castelo. The remarkable architectural landmarks in the area, which represent many historical eras, demonstrate the neighbourhood's historical significance.

  Oliveira do Castelo captures the core of Portugal's transformation as a nation, from its mediaeval origins to its later alterations.

- **Oliveira do Castelo Church:** The Oliveira do Castelo Church is one of the neighbourhood's most distinctive features. This religious monument is a work of architecture that perfectly illustrates how several styles may coexist. The church, which incorporates aspects of Gothic,

Manueline, and Baroque design, acts as a physical illustration of the area's varied cultural background.

- The Guimaraes City Hall, which is located in Oliveira do Castelo, is a shining example of how history and modernity can coexist. The structure combines its historical original components with modern modifications to produce a distinctive architectural fusion that exemplifies the city's dedication to conserving its history while embracing its present.

Cultural Celebrations and Events:

- Cultural activities and celebrations bring Oliveira do Castelo to life as they honour the area's history and present-day energy. The area hosts numerous events all year long that bring together residents and guests to enjoy life and the vibrant cultural diversity of the city.

- The Gualterianas festival, which is held in honour of Saint Gualter, is one of Oliveira do Castelo's most eagerly awaited festivals. The festival is filled with joyful street festivals, energetic processions, and traditional music that transports attendees back in time.

Contemporary Culture and Art:

- Oliveira do Castelo is grounded in history but also embraces the modern arts and cultural environment. The galleries and cultural centres that hold a wide variety of exhibitions, performances, and activities that highlight contemporary artistic expression and innovation are open to visitors.

- Centro Cultural Vila Flor is a vibrant centre for artistic expression and cultural events, and it is close by. The centre holds a variety of activities, such as art exhibitions, theatrical productions, concerts, and workshops, and also attracts talent from outside of Portugal.

- **Modern Architecture:** The neighbourhood's architectural landscape also includes cutting-edge styles that harmoniously blend with the older buildings. The fusion of the old and new creates an intriguing contrast that highlights the city's progression through time and embracing modern living.

Conclusion:

The area of Oliveira do Castelo, where history and modernity collide, enthrals visitors with its rich cultural past and energetic current. Guimaraes has been transforming into a city that values its past while embracing the promise of the future as one visits its historical sites, participates in cultural events, and experiences the current art scene.

Oliveira do Castelo is a must-visit location for tourists looking for a genuine and magical experience in the heart of Guimaraes because time there seems to flow effortlessly, crafting a mesmerising tale that ties the threads of Portugal's history and culture together.

Creixomil: Embracing Nature And Tranquility

Creixomil: Embracing Tranquility and Nature Creixomil is a peaceful neighbourhood that embraces the beauty of nature and provides a relaxing retreat from the busy city centre. It is tucked away in the magnificent terrain of Guimaraes.

Creixomil welcomes visitors to immerse themselves in the calming embrace of nature because it is surrounded by lush vegetation, rolling hills, and serene parks.

Creixomil is a destination for individuals looking for leisure, outdoor experiences, and a revitalising connection with nature thanks to its gorgeous surroundings and friendly community.

Penha Mountain: A Green Haven

- Penha Mountain, a magnificent natural sanctuary that enthrals visitors with its beauty and biodiversity, is located in the centre of Creixomil. Penha Mountain, one of Guimaraes' most well-known sights, is a haven for hikers and environment lovers.

Its vast network of trails allows you to explore the area's natural beauties and take in the peace of the outdoors while also providing access to beautiful vistas, secret caverns, and cool waterfalls.

Guimaraes City Park: A Calm Sanctuary

- Guimaraes City Park, a wonderful urban oasis that provides the ideal backdrop for leisurely walks, picnics, and periods of calm thought, is close to

Penha Mountain. Visitors are encouraged to relax and get in touch with nature through the park's well-kept gardens, shady walkways, and tranquil lakes.

Families frequently congregate here for fun vacations, and tourists frequently see residents playing friendly games or just taking in the scenery.

The Coexistence of Natural Environment and Cultural Heritage

- While Creixomil is well known for its natural wonders, it also has a thriving cultural history that complements its lush surroundings. Visitors can find historical sites that honour the neighbourhood's heritage and capture the resilient character of the area amidst the lush flora.

- Chapel of Saint Martinho: The Chapel of Saint Martinho is a historic religious site that dates back to the 12th century and is a treasure concealed among the natural beauties. Its appealing architectural features and serene atmosphere make it a welcoming setting for reflecting and appreciating Creixomil's spiritual and cultural heritage.

- Chapel of Senhor do Socorro: The Chapel of Senhor do Socorro is a historical landmark that adds to the neighbourhood's cultural value.

    Its charming charm and religious significance provide a window into Guimaraes' customary practices and spiritual fervour.

A Sanctuary for Rest and Rejuvenation

- The tranquillity and embrace of nature in Creixomil make it the perfect location for therapeutic activities like retreats and meditation.

  The tranquil ambiance of the area provides a respite from the stress of daily life, allowing guests to find comfort in the beauty of their surroundings and reclaim their inner serenity.

Activities and Adventures in the Natural World

- Creixomil provides a wide range of outdoor adventure activities that are grounded in the natural world. Nature lovers can enjoy birding and the region's unique flora and wildlife, while hikers can explore the beautiful paths of Penha Mountain.

Conclusion

With its embrace of quiet and nature, Creixomil is a haven of peace in the centre of Guimaraes. The lush surroundings of Penha Mountain and the tranquil haven of Guimaraes City Park provide a restorative respite for guests looking to re-establish a connection with nature and achieve inner serenity.

Creixomil is a hidden gem that lures visitors to enjoy moments of peace, adventure, and soulful reflection because of the synergy between natural beauty and cultural legacy.

IMMERSING IN GUIMARAES' CULTURE

Festivals and Events: Celebrations Not to Miss

Events and Festivals You Shouldn't Miss

With its thriving cultural scene and upbeat attitude, Guimaraes holds a wide range of festivals and events all year long that honour the city's rich past, artistic expression, and zest for life.

These festivals offer a thrilling experience for both locals and tourists, with historical reenactments that transport visitors to mediaeval times and contemporary art exhibitions that highlight modern innovation. Avoid missing these festive events that bring colour and excitement to Guimaraes' cultural calendar when you go there:

1. **Gualterianas Festival**: The Gualterianas Festival, which takes place in August, is one of Guimaraes' most eagerly awaited occasions. The event, which is named after Saint Gualter, the patron saint of the city, includes vivacious parades, performances of traditional music and dance, as well as a bustling market that evokes the Middle Ages.

   Visitors can immerse themselves in Guimaraes' past through historical reenactments and processions dressed historically.

2. **White Night (Noite Branca)**: During the White Night celebration in September, Guimaraes is transformed into a captivating nocturnal wonderland. Streets, public spaces, and significant sites in the city serve as outdoor

platforms for creative performances, light works, and hands-on exhibits. This festival of contemporary art and culture gives the city fresh energy and offers a spectacular experience that highlights contemporary creativity.

3. **Festas Gualterianas da Cidade Pequena:** This neighbourhood celebration honours Saint Gualter with a vibrant procession and a fun fair featuring live music, regional cuisine, and handcrafted goods. It is a favourite among both locals and tourists because of the jovial mood and unique customs.

4. **Festival Manta:** This colourful event, which honours folk music and dancing in numerous sites throughout Guimaraes, is known as Festival Manta. A vibrant and varied cultural experience is created when musicians and dancers from Portugal and other

nations join together to share their cultural heritage and showcase their talents.

5. **Festas Nicolinas:** Dating back to the 14th century, the Festas Nicolinas is a historic and rowdy event that takes place in late November and early December. The celebrations, which are named after Saint Nicholas, feature vibrant parades, music, dancing, and merry street parties. The "Pinheiro," a big tree that locals compete to steal from one another in good fun, is the highlight.

6. **Natal no Centro Histórico**: Christmas in Guimaraes is a magical time to travel there. Christmas markets, concerts, and cultural events fill the streets of the old district, which is decked out in festive décor. Families and guests will love the cosy and welcoming feeling

that the Christmas lights and decor provide.

7. **Guimaraes Jazz Festival:** The Guimaraes Jazz Festival is a must-attend event for jazz lovers. Renowned jazz musicians congregate to perform at a variety of locations throughout the city, mesmerising listeners with beautiful melodies and improvisation.

Jazz enthusiasts will have a wonderful experience thanks to the festival's cosy settings.

8. **Carnival:** The Guimaraes Carnival festivities are a riot of hues, garb, and fun. Both locals and tourists wear imaginative costumes as they dance and sing to upbeat rhythms on the streets. Parades, street performances,

and events that celebrate and have fun bring the city to life.

Conclusion

Celebrations play a crucial role in Guimaraes' cultural identity, offering a variety of activities that pay homage to the city's rich history, diverse creative heritage, and welcoming atmosphere.

Every tourist will find something to pique their interest at Guimaraes' festivals and events, whether they are drawn to the exuberant rhythms of music and dance, modern art, or historical reenactments.

In addition to being fun, these events offer a special chance to interact with the neighbourhood, learn about the local customs, and cement lifelong memories of a memorable cultural encounter.

Gastronomy and Culinary Delights: Must-Try Dishes and Restaurants

Gastronomy and culinary delights: dishes and eateries you Must Try

In addition to being rich in history and culture, Guimaraes is a destination for foodies looking to indulge in traditional Portuguese fare and gourmet treats. The city's cuisine features a variety of tastes and recipes that highlight regional delicacies and local ingredients, reflecting its rich cultural background.

For an outstanding dining experience while exploring Guimaraes, be sure to sample these meals at some of the city's top restaurants:

1. **Caldo Verde**: Caldo Verde, a traditional Portuguese cuisine, is a warming soup made with cabbage and potatoes. Slices of the spicy sausage "chouriço,"

which is made with love in Guimaraes, are added to this classic soup to give it an extra flavorful bite. On chilly days, Caldo Verde is ideal for keeping warm while enjoying the real flavour of Portuguese comfort food.

2. **Bacalhau com Broa**: In Guimaraes, a traditional Portuguese dish called , or salted codfish, is made in a special and mouthwatering fashion. A lovely combination of tastes and textures is produced in this meal by topping codfish with a cornbread crumb crust. It's a seafood lover's must-try and a showcase for the area's inventive cooking.

3. **Pudim Abade de Priscos**: Pudim Abade de Priscos is a dessert lover's dream come true. With eggs, sugar, bacon, and Port wine, this thick and velvety pudding has a distinctive and decadent

flavour profile. This dessert is a delicious way to end any dinner and is typically served with a drizzle of sweet syrup.

4. **Francesinha**: Although it is not a native food of Guimaraes, Francesinha has grown to be a beloved dish there, and discovering an authentic rendition is a treat.

This filling sandwich is covered with melty cheese, a luscious tomato and beer sauce, and layers of meats like steak, ham, and sausage. It goes nicely with a cool beer and is frequently served with a side of fries.

5. **Rojes à Minhota:** Rojes are tender pork cubes that are slow-cooked to perfection. They are tasty. They are frequently served in Guimaraes with "arroz de sarrabulho," a rice dish made

with pork blood, making for an unusual and flavorful pairing that is sure to please meat aficionados.

Best Restaurants to Sample Guimaraes' Cuisine:

1. **Restaurante Fentastic:** Located in Guimaraes, Restaurante Fentastic is well-known for its hearty hospitality and traditional Portuguese cuisine. Regional specialties, seafood, and beef meals are all offered on their comprehensive menu, which is made with only the best, freshest ingredients.

2. **Restaurante Largo do Toural**: This quaint eatery, which is located in the city's historic district, serves up both regional and foreign cuisine. It's a great option for anyone who wants to enjoy traditional Portuguese flavours with a contemporary touch.

3. Restaurante Histórico by Papaboa: Located in a lovely old structure, Restaurante Histórico by Papaboa offers a delicious gastronomic experience with an emphasis on seasonal and local products. The presentation of their food is exquisite, and the hospitable ambiance of the restaurant enhances the overall dining experience.

4. **Restaurant Muralha:** This charming establishment offers a setting with views of the old city walls and is close to Guimaraes Castle. Traditional Portuguese food is served in the restaurant, with a focus on fresh fish and grilled meats.

5. **Tasquinha da Linda**: This undiscovered gem offers a genuine flavour of local cuisine. This family-run eatery serves

handcrafted cuisine that highlights the genuine flavours of Guimaraes in a warm and welcoming setting.

Conclusion: A Guimaraes Gastronomic Adventure

The cuisine of Guimaraes is a gourmet excursion where traditional recipes and inventive cooking join together to provide a pleasurable experience for food lovers. Each meal shows a different aspect of Portugal's gastronomic history, from the filling Caldo Verde to the decadent Pudim Abade de Priscos.

Travellers can experience the finest flavours of Guimaraes while soaking in the warm hospitality and vibrant culture that make the city an unbeatable setting for culinary exploration by dining at the city's top restaurants.

Traditional Crafts: Shopping for Local Artisanal Products

For those looking to shop for regional artisanal goods and traditional crafts, Guimaraes is a treasure trove because of its rich cultural heritage and passion for craftsmanship.

Craftspeople in the city continue to use traditional methods to produce authentic one-of-a-kind items and reflect the local culture. Be sure to look at these conventional crafts and handcrafted goods when shopping in Guimaraes:

1. **Ceramics**: Guimaraes is well known for its exquisite ceramics, which are produced in a range of styles, including pottery, dinnerware, and ornamental tiles. Find delicately painted tiles, vibrant vases, and other works of art that highlight the city's artistic talent

by visiting nearby workshops and businesses.

2. Jewellery crafted in the ancient art of filigree, which uses fine metalwork to produce elaborate jewellery items. Exquisite filigree necklaces, earrings, and bracelets, frequently with traditional Portuguese themes and patterns, are available in Guimaraes.

3. **Lacework and embroidery:** The city's lacework and embroidery are evidence of its commitment to maintaining conventional workmanship. To add a sense of luxury to any home, look around your neighbourhood for handcrafted lace tablecloths, napkins, and embroidered linens.

4. **Wooden Carvings:** Another highly regarded art in Guimaraes is the meticulous carving of figures,

sculptures, and ornamental objects. These wooden sculptures frequently include historical characters, religious icons, and folkloric scenes from Portugal.

5. **Leather Products**: Guimaraes is renowned for its fine leather craftsmanship, creating leather accessories such as wallets, belts, and bags. Look for leather artists that make high-quality, fashionable things using age-old methods.

6. **Traditional Textiles:** Discover one-of-a-kind items crafted from regionally sourced fibres while exploring Guimaraes' rich textile traditions. Discover the city's commitment to preserving its textile legacy by looking for woven rugs, blankets, and traditional clothes.

7. **Cork Products:** Guimaraes takes pride in using this sustainable material to create a variety of products. Portugal is one of the world's top cork producers. You can find a wide variety of cork-based crafts, including wallets, keychains, and home decor.

8. **Pottery**: Making pottery is a long-standing tradition in Guimaraes. You may find exquisitely handcrafted pottery that combines modern designs with age-old methods. Look for attractive plates, cups, and bowls that can be used and look good.

9. **Handwoven Baskets**: Using natural fibres, skilled local weavers create distinctive and useful products that can be used for shopping, storage, or decoration.

10. **Classic Toys:** Look for classic wooden toys like spinning tops, wooden puzzles, and dolls that are all lovingly handcrafted if you want to find something special to bring back for the little ones in your life.

What to Buy:

1. **Centro Cultural Vila Flor**: You may engage with local artisans in-person and buy their works of art during craft fairs and artisan markets held frequently at this cultural centre.

2. **Mercado Municipal de Guimaraes**: The municipal market is an excellent location to find a wide range of locally made goods, including artisanal goods and conventional crafts.

3. **Artisan Workshops:** Wander the city's neighbourhoods in search of tiny

stores and workshops where local craftspeople sell their handmade wares to tourists.

4. **Rua de Santa Maria**: Lined with quaint shops and boutiques, some of which specialise in age-old arts and crafts and handmade goods, this street is a great place to browse.

In summary, Guimaraes is honouring artistic excellence.

Shopping for regional artisanal goods in Guimaraes is an opportunity to not only locate one-of-a-kind trinkets but also to celebrate the city's rich cultural heritage and love of fine craftsmanship.

You'll come across a variety of traditional crafts and artistic products that capture the spirit of Guimaraes as you explore the markets, stores, and workshops. You may contribute to preserving the city's artistic past for future generations by buying these genuine items and supporting local craftspeople.

OUTDOOR ADVENTURES IN GUIMARAES

Guimaraes provides a wide range of outdoor excursions for nature lovers and adventure seekers alike thanks to its alluring natural surroundings and stunning sceneries.

The city invites visitors to immerse themselves in the splendour of the outdoors and discover the wonders of nature by trekking up Penha Mountain, taking a leisurely lunch in Guimaraes City Park, and going on bike tours of the surrounding area.

Penha Mountain: Exciting Hiking and Magnificent Views

- Penha Mountain is a refuge for hikers and environment enthusiasts and stands as an iconic natural feature overlooking Guimaraes. Adventurers who climb Penha Mountain are rewarded with breathtaking panoramas of the city and the surrounding region. The network of clearly marked routes on the mountain provides a variety of trekking opportunities for both novice and expert hikers. Discover scenic locations, secret caverns, and rich foliage along the way to make the journey as magical as the destination.

Guimaraes City Park: Relaxation and Picnics

- Guimaraes City Park, a calm urban oasis close to Penha Mountain, welcomes visitors to repose and unwind in its serene surroundings.

The quiet atmosphere of the park, which is ideal for leisurely walks and picnics, is created by its well-kept gardens, shady trails, and tranquil lake. Families frequently congregate here for fun vacations, and tourists frequently see residents playing friendly games or just taking in the scenery. Guimaraes City Park offers a revitalising retreat from the city's bustle, whether it's a stroll or a pleasant picnic with loved ones.

Exploring the Surrounding Countryside on Cycling Tours

- Guimaraes provides thrilling bicycle experiences that let guests immerse themselves in the natural beauty of the nearby region for those who like to explore on two wheels.

  Cycle through quaint towns, wineries, and stunning vistas as you travel through scenic trails and backroads. The region's varied terrains are suitable for riders of all experience levels, whether they are ardent cyclists or casual riders. Cycling excursions offer a singular chance to see the genuine charm of the countryside while embracing the sense of freedom that comes with being outside.

Sports and Activities for Adventure

- For those looking for an adrenaline rush, Guimaraes also provides a variety of adventure sports and activities. Rock climbing, zip lining, and paragliding are choices for thrill-seekers, allowing you to observe the area from spectacular vantage points.

    In addition, surrounding rivers provide kayaking and rafting options, making them a refreshing getaway during the warmer months.

In Guimaraes, embrace the great outdoors.

Outdoor activities in Guimaraes provide the ideal blend of breathtaking scenery, tranquillity, and exhilarating thrills. The city is a haven for outdoor enthusiasts, whether you're climbing up Penha Mountain to take in the stunning views, having a leisurely picnic in Guimaraes City Park, or going on bicycle trips through the lovely countryside.

Engaging in outdoor activities in Guimaraes offers the ability to reconnect with nature as well as to refresh the body, mind, and soul while making lifelong memories of an outstanding outdoor journey in this culturally significant region of Portugal.

DAY TRIPS FROM GUIMARAES

Braga: A Pilgrimage to Portugal's Religious Capital

Braga: A Visit to Portugal's Spiritual Centre

Braga, which is located in northern Portugal, is a place rich in spiritual significance and religious heritage.

Braga, also referred to as the "Rome of Portugal," is home to numerous mediaeval churches, sacred monuments, and other places of worship, earning it the title of the nation's religious capital.

Braga provides a pilgrimage of immense cultural and historical value for those looking for a closer spiritual connection and a glimpse into Portugal's religious legacy.

The Sé Cathedral serves as Braga's spiritual centre.

- The beautiful 12th-century Roman Catholic church known as the Sé Cathedral sits in the middle of Braga's spiritual environment. The cathedral is awe-inspiring to view due to its majesty and architectural brilliance.

    Visitors can tour the Chapel of the Kings, which is inside, as well as the treasury, which contains priceless religious goods and valuables.

    Both are decorated with elaborate carvings and historical tombs. Anyone making a pilgrimage to Braga should see the Sé Cathedral, which represents the city's strong religious identity.

Bom Jesus do Monte Sanctuary: A Path to Spirituality

- The Sanctuary of Bom Jesus do Monte is one of Braga's most recognizable landmarks, and it's only a short walk from the city centre. This holy place is well-known for its 577-step Baroque staircase that leads to the sanctuary. On their knees, pilgrims climb the staircase in penance and devotion.

The sanctuary's vantage point at the top provides amazing views of Braga and its surroundings.

The trip to Bom Jesus do Monte is a genuinely spiritual and fulfilling experience because of the sanctuary's majestic cathedral and ornate chapels, which are equally worth examining.

São Martinho de Dume: Discovering the Christian Origins

- São Martinho de Dume, the former archbishopric of Braga and one of the oldest Christian churches in Portugal, is another important religious site in the city.

This ancient religious complex has a significant historical significance and dates to the fourth century. Visitors can trace the beginnings of Christianity in Portugal and see the remains of an early Christian community by seeing the So Martinho de Dume ruins.

Churches and chapels are additional religious treasures.

- There are countless further churches and chapels in Braga, each with a distinct religious significance and history. Among the prominent religious locations well worth visiting are the Church of Santa Cruz, with its lovely exterior and Baroque interior, and the Church of San Marcos, famed for its superb tiles and azulejos. A serene haven of devotion, the Chapel of So Frutuoso is located amidst lush gardens.

Religious Holidays and Festivities

- Religious festivals and celebrations take place all year long in Braga, drawing pilgrims and tourists from far and wide.

  Holy Week, also known as Semana Santa, is marked by religious celebrations and processions that honour Christ's suffering on the cross. Other cheerful celebrations that combine religious traditions with cultural activities include Festas de So Joo.

A Journey of Faith and Heritage, Conclusion

- The city's spiritual sites and religious customs provide an enthralling voyage of religion and legacy, earning Braga the distinction of Portugal's religious capital.

  Each step taken in Braga brings tourists closer to the core of Portugal's religious identity, whether they are ascending the stairs of Bom Jesus do Monte or visiting the historic remains of So Martinho de Dume.

The city is a pilgrimage destination that affects the soul and leaves a lasting impression on everyone who undertakes this sacred journey thanks to its rich history, architectural riches, and exciting religious festivals.

Amarante: A Riverside Escape

A Riverside Escape, Amarante

Amarante, a quaint riverside village in northern Portugal, is tucked away along the banks of the Tâmega River and makes for an exquisite getaway for tourists looking for a slower pace of life and a taste of traditional Portuguese culture.

Amarante invites tourists to immerse themselves in the beauty of its surroundings and unwind in the calm of the river's embrace with its stunning scenery, antique buildings, and kind hospitality.

A Trip Through Time at the Historic Centre

- The historic district of Amarante is a charming labyrinth of cobblestone lanes lined with well-maintained structures that display a variety of architectural styles, from Baroque to Romanesque.

    The So Gonçalo Church and Monastery, which represents dedication and religion in the area, is one church that reflects the town's rich history.

    Discover the cultural richness that has influenced Amarante over the years by strolling around the attractive squares, going to nearby museums, and exploring historical sites.

Riverside Strolls: Appreciating the Beauty of Nature

- The Tâmega River is Amarante's lifeblood, and everybody visiting the town must take a stroll along its banks. You may find picturesque, tree-shaded walking pathways along the riverbanks, which are ideal for strolls and quiet times.

Take pictures of the river, the historic Ponte São Gonçalo bridge, and the quaint buildings that dot the countryside. The quiet atmosphere of the riverbank offers a tranquil backdrop for unwinding and connecting with nature.

Enjoying the Flavors of Amarante's Cuisine

- The cuisine of Amarante is a celebration of real Portuguese flavours, with age-old recipes honouring the area's rich gastronomic history. Enjoy regional specialties like "papas de anjo" (heavenly egg-based pastries), "roles" (marinated pork), and "sardines de escabeche" (marinated sardines).

Don't forget to accompany your dinner with a glass of Vinho Verde, a light and refreshing wine made locally that goes well with the flavours of Amarante's food.

Amarante Water Park: A Fun Family Attraction

- The Amarante Water Park offers a fun-filled day of water slides, pools, and games for people seeking family-friendly entertainment. This water park is close to the town and is well-liked by both inhabitants and visitors, especially in the hot summer months. The cool pools and lush green surrounds of the water park provide the ideal relief from the summer heat.

Festivals and Events: Culture and Traditions

- Amarante comes alive with festivals and activities that highlight the community's rich traditions and sense of civic pride. The town's patron saint is honoured during the Festas de São Gonçalo, which takes place in June. Parades, music, dancing, and a cheerful fair are all part of the celebrations, which draw people from all over the area to attend.

  The occasion is a wonderful chance to enjoy Amarante's kind hospitality and become fully immersed in the spirit of community.

An Enduring Riverside Haven

For those seeking a tranquil escape from the hustle and bustle of contemporary life, Amarante's riverside getaway is the right location because it offers the ultimate fusion of history, nature, and culture.

Amarante welcomes you to appreciate the beauty and peace of its riverfront charm, whether strolling along the riverbanks, indulging in the delicacies of Portuguese cuisine, or immersing yourself in the town's rich tradition. Everyone who visits the coastline of this picture-perfect village will have a memorable and relaxing experience.

Douro Valley: Wine Tasting Amidst Vineyard

Wine tasting in the Douro Valley amidst vineyards

The Douro Valley, a gorgeous wine region in northern Portugal noted for producing some of the world's best wines, is tucked between undulating hills and terraced vines.

Wine lovers and tourists looking to indulge in the craft of winemaking amid spectacular natural beauty will find a mesmerising escape at this UNESCO World Heritage Site.

The Douro Valley offers an amazing wine-centric experience, including vineyard tours, wine tastings, and picturesque cruises along the Douro River.

Terraced Vineyards: Evidence of Winemaking Expertise

- Terraced vineyards, an inventive and age-old agricultural technique that produces stunning panoramas, are well-known in the Douro Valley. These terraces, which were carved into the hillsides, maximise sun exposure, enabling the vines to thrive in the area's microclimates.

 You will see the dedication and skill that go into creating some of the world's best wines as you meander through the vines under the guidance of local winemakers.

Wine Tours: Exploring Special Flavours

- Without partaking in wine-tasting sessions at the Quintas (wineries) in the region, a trip to the Douro Valley would be incomplete. From strong reds to crisp whites and the well-known Port wine, each Quinta provides a distinctive assortment of wines. Learn about the winemaking process and the various grape varieties that prosper in the Douro Valley while savouring the aromas of the region's terroir.

Many wineries now provide food pairings, giving patrons the chance to enjoy regional delicacies along with their wines.

Douro River Cruises: Beautiful Water Views

- Take a leisurely river trip along the Douro River to get a different view of the Douro Valley's splendour. Enjoy the breathtaking views of the terraced vineyards, quaint villages, and historic stone bridges that border the riverbanks from the deck of a traditional Rabelo boat. The tranquillity of the water adds to the enjoyment of this magical place as you cruise through the valley, where the beauty unfolds like a canvas.

Harvest Time: A Festive Season

- In the Douro Valley, festivities take place throughout the harvest season, which normally lasts from September to October. When the grapes are hand-picked, vineyards come alive with celebrations and customs involving the stomping of grapes.

  A unique opportunity to experience the winemaking process at its most lively and to take part in the festive mood of the grape harvest is to travel during the harvest season.

Exploring Wine Heritage through Wine Museums and Interpretive Centers

- Visit the area's wine museums and interpretive centres to learn more about the history and culture of winemaking in the Douro Valley. These organisations provide information about the viticultural history, long-standing customs, and technological advancements that have influenced the local wine business.

Conclusion: A Memorable Wine Adventure

The wine-tasting excursion in the Douro Valley is an adventure that enchants the senses and enthrals the soul.

Travellers are treated to a unique wine-focused trip set amidst terraced vineyards, vintage wineries, and the serene Douro River. The winemakers of the Douro

Valley impart not only their knowledge but also their love for what they do, creating a friendly atmosphere that makes visitors to this haven for wine lovers feel welcome and at home. The Douro Valley promises a wine trip that will take your appreciation of wine to new heights, regardless of whether you are an experienced wine expert or an enthusiastic novice.

PRACTICAL TIPS FOR A SMOOTH TRIP

Transportation Options: Getting Around Guimaraes

Since Guimaraes is a small, well-connected city, getting about is not too difficult. There are several ways to explore the city and its surroundings, whether you like to walk through the picturesque streets or take public transportation.

1. Walking: Guimaraes' historic core is a pleasure to explore on foot because it is pedestrian-friendly.

   The Guimaraes Castle and the Palace of the Dukes of Braganza are only two of the city's many attractions that are close to one another. You may take in the atmosphere of the city and find hidden treasures while ambling over the cobblestone streets.

2. **Buses**: The TUG (Transportes Urbanos de Guimaraes) operates a dependable bus network in Guimaraes. Bus routes run throughout the city and its environs, making it simple to get to various neighbourhoods and attractions. Bus tickets can be purchased at ticket booths or while on the bus itself.

3. **Taxis**: If you don't like to travel great distances, taxis are a convenient and pleasant way to get around the city and are widely available in Guimaraes. Taxis are available at specialised taxi stands or can be flagged down on the street.

4. **Car Rental**: Renting a car is a wonderful choice if you want to explore the surrounding area and

neighbouring attractions at your own pace. In Guimaraes, there are several vehicle rental companies, and having a car gives you the freedom to travel outside of the city.

5. **Renting a bicycle:** This is a great option for eco-friendly and unhurried exploring. You can rent a bicycle from some hotels or neighbourhood stores and pedal through the city and along the neighbouring bike lanes while taking your time to take in the beauty.

6. **Trains**: Although Guimaraes lacks a train station of its own, the neighbouring city of Porto has excellent train service to numerous locations all across Portugal. You can travel to Guimaraes by train from Porto for a day excursion or to see the city's historical landmarks.

Getting Around Advice:

- Since Guimaraes is a tiny city, most attractions are accessible by foot. For touring the cobblestone streets and hilly landscape, put on some comfy shoes.

- Consider buying a rechargeable Andante card, which can be used on buses and trains in the Porto metropolitan region, including Guimaraes, if you want to use public transit regularly.

- Taxis might be a practical choice for short journeys or late-night rides back to your lodging.

To discover more about the historical and cultural sites of the city, take advantage of guided walking tours.

Overall, moving around Guimaraes is a pleasant experience that enables you to easily explore the city's attractions and immerse yourself in its historical charm.

Accommodations: Where to Stay for Every Budget

Guimaraes provides a range of lodging choices to fit any budget, from opulent hotels to comfortable guesthouses and affordable hostels.

Every traveller can find the ideal spot to stay, whether they like to stay in the historic district or a quiet area outside the city.

Following are some lodging choices to take into account based on your budget:

Luxurious lodging:

- The Guimaraes Castle's inner walls house the luxurious Pousada Mosteiro de Guimarães, which provides breathtaking views of the city and its surroundings. The hotel offers a distinctive and opulent experience because it is set in a gorgeously restored monastery from the 12th century.

- Santa Luzia Arthotel is a chic hotel with contemporary decor that is conveniently located close to the city centre. The rooftop patio is a wonderful place to relax and take in the surroundings because it offers sweeping views of Guimaraes.

- The historic district's boutique hotel, Hotel da Oliveira, offers opulent rooms decorated in classic Portuguese style. The hotel's convenient location makes it simple to visit Guimaraes' top restaurants and sights.

Medium-Priced Accommodation:

- **Hotel Toural:** This mid-range hotel is located in Guimaraes' central plaza and offers welcoming rooms with contemporary conveniences. The city's sights and cultural sites are easily accessible due to the location's centrality.

- **Hotel Fundador:** Situated in a quiet neighbourhood just outside the city centre, this hotel provides a relaxing refuge while still being close to the main sights.

- **Stay at Hotel Guimaraes Centro**: This hotel offers clean, comfortable rooms at a reasonable price in the heart of the city. For tourists seeking both convenience and value, it's a fantastic option.

Easily Affordable Accommodation:

- Located in the city's historic district, Hostel Prime Guimaraes provides affordable individual rooms as well as dormitory-style lodging. Budget and backpackers alike frequently choose it.

- **Hostel Fa**: This hostel offers reasonably priced individual and dorm rooms close to the Guimaraes train station. For people searching for affordable lodging who are arriving by rail, it is a practical choice.

- **Residencial dos Carvalhais**: This inn provides straightforward, cosy accommodations at reasonable costs. It's a wonderful option for tourists looking for a comfortable and inexpensive hotel.

Vacation rentals and Airbnb:

- Consider renting a vacation home or staying in an Airbnb in Guimaraes for a more individualised experience. You can live like a local and enjoy the luxuries of a home away from home by choosing one of the many apartments and houses that are available for short-term visits.

Summary: A Wide Variety of Accommodations

With its extensive selection of lodging options, Guimaraes can accommodate travellers of all financial abilities. You'll discover the ideal location to stay for an unforgettable visit to this historic jewel of Portugal, whether you like luxury hotels with breathtaking views, beautiful mid-range hotels in the centre of the city, or cost-effective hostels and guesthouses.

Plan and reserve your lodging early, especially during the busiest travel times, to get the best prices and have a relaxing stay while visiting Guimaraes.

Safety and Health: Staying Well-informed

To guarantee a smooth and pleasurable journey, it's important to keep aware of safety and health issues before travelling to Guimaraes or any other location. Here are some pointers to keep you secure and healthy while you're there:

1. **Travel insurance**: Make sure you have sufficient travel insurance that covers medical emergencies, trip cancellations, and other unforeseen situations before you depart for Guimaraes. A sense of security and financial security in the event of any unanticipated circumstances are provided by travel insurance.

2. **Health Precautions**: Before your trip, make sure you are up to date on standard vaccinations and discuss any

additional immunizations or health precautions you might need for Portugal with your doctor or a travel health centre. Maintain a copy of your medical records and carry any essential prescriptions and medications with you at all times.

3. **COVID-19 Safety Measures**: Keep up with the most recent COVID-19 restrictions and standards in Guimaraes. For the most updated travel warnings and health precautions, consult the World Health Organization (WHO) and official government websites.

4. Save the local emergency contact information for the police, ambulance, and closest hospital in your phone. All crises in Portugal should be reported by calling the emergency number, which is 112.

5. **Preventing Petty Theft:** Take precautions with your possessions and avoid travelling with significant sums of cash or valuables, just like you would in any tourist location. In a hotel safe, store your money, passport, and other valuables. Due to the prevalence of petty theft in congested areas and on public transportation, exercise caution there.

6. Tap water is generally safe to consume across Portugal, including Guimaraes. However, bottled water is frequently offered for purchase if you want it.

7. **Food safety**: Savour the regional fare, but use caution while eating uncooked or raw foods. Eat at respected establishments and observe fundamental food hygiene rules.

8. **Respect Local Customs:** To demonstrate respect for the regional culture and traditions, become familiar with local customs and etiquette. When visiting places of worship, dress appropriately and be aware of regional traditions.

9. **Road Safety:** Get acquainted with local traffic laws and road restrictions if you intend to drive or take public transportation. When crossing the street, proceed with caution and heed all pedestrian lights and crosswalks.

10. **Sun protection:** Guimaraes experiences a Mediterranean climate, and the sun may be intense, particularly in the summer. To avoid sunburn and illnesses brought on by the heat, wear sunscreen, sunglasses, and a hat.

In conclusion, travel responsibly and safely.

You may have a safe and happy trip to Guimaraes by being aware and following the appropriate safety precautions. Respect the culture of the area, take good care of your health, and stay informed of any safety or health recommendations.

Enjoy this historic city's beauty and charm while travelling properly and looking out for your well-being at all times.

Additional Resources and Websites

Here are some more resources and websites to consider as you continue to research Guimaraes and Portugal:

1. **Visit Portugal:** The official website of the Portuguese Tourism Board offers detailed information about locations, points of interest, events, and helpful travel advice for the entire nation. Visit Portugal's website at:

2. **Guimaraes Tourism:** The organisation's official website provides comprehensive information about the city's attractions, activities, lodging options, and more. the website guimaraesturismo.com

3. The Lonely Planet website offers travel information, advice, and travel guides for Portugal, including Guimaraes. Visit

the website at www.lonelyplanet.com/portugal

4. **TripAdvisor - Guimaraes**: Guimaraes attractions, restaurants, and lodging are covered by reviews, rankings, and traveller photos on TripAdvisor. www.tripadvisor.com/Guimaraes is the website.

5. **The official Douro Valley Website**: Visit the official website for more details about the Douro Valley, including wine excursions and river cruises. Website address: durovalley. eu

6. **Official Tourism Website of Lisbon**: If you intend to travel to Lisbon or the southern regions, this website is a great resource. URL: www.visitlisboa.com

7. **Camino de Santiago:** The official website offers information about the Camino de Santiago pilgrimage route as well as resources and travel preparation tools. Visit the website at www.caminodesantiago.gal/en

8. **Worldwide Organization for Health (WHO):** Check the WHO website frequently for the latest health cautions and suggestions, especially during the COVID-19 epidemic. Visit the WHO website.

Always make sure any website or resource you utilise for trip planning is reliable and trustworthy. In general, reputable travel guides and official tourism websites are trustworthy sources of information.

Enjoy your vacation discovering Guimaraes and all that Portugal has to offer while travelling safely! Feel free to ask any more questions or for help if you need it. Happy travels!

LANGUAGE AND USEFUL PHRASES

Basic Portuguese Expressions for Travelers

Knowing some fundamental Portuguese phrases can be immensely useful in day-to-day interactions as a traveller in Portugal. Your efforts will be valued by the locals, and it may improve your trip as a whole. The following are some crucial Portuguese phrases for travellers:

1. Hello: Olá (oh-LAH)
2. Good morning: Bom dia (bohm DEE-ah)
3. Good afternoon: Boa tarde (boh-ah TAR-deh)
4. Good evening/night: Boa noite (boh-ah NOY-teh)
5. Please: Por favor (pohr fah-VOHR)

6. Thank you: Obrigado (if you're male) / Obrigada (if you're female) (oh-bree-GAH-doo / oh-bree-GAH-dah)
7. You're welcome: De nada (dee NAH-dah)
8. Yes: Sim (seeng)
9. No: Não (now)
10. Excuse me / Sorry: Desculpe (deh-SKOO-pee)
11. I don't understand: Não entendo (now ehn-TEHN-doo)
12. Do you speak English?: Fala inglês? (FAH-lah een-GLAYS?)
13. I need help: Preciso de ajuda (preh-SEE-zoo dee ah-ZOOL-dah)
14. How much is this?: Quanto custa isso? (KWAHN-too KOOSH-tah EE-soo?)
15. Where is...?: Onde fica...? (OHN-dee FEE-kah...?)
16. Bathroom: Casa de banho (KAH-sah deh BAH-nyoo)

17. I would like...: Gostaria de... (go-STAH-ree-ah deh...)
18. Can I have the check, please?: A conta, por favor (ah KOHN-tah, pohr fah-VOHR)

Useful Travel Phrases:

1. I am a tourist: Sou turista (soh too-REES-tah)

2. Can you take a photo of me?: Pode tirar uma foto de mim? (POH-deh tee-RAHR OO-mah FOH-toh deh meem?)

3. Where is the nearest metro/bus station?: Onde fica a estação de metro/ônibus mais próxima? (OHN-deh FEE-kah ah eh-stah-SOW deh MAY-troh / OHN-ee-boos mah-ees NOH-mah FEE-kah?)

4. I'd like a table for two, please: Gostaria de uma mesa para dois, por favor (go-STAH-ree-ah deh OO-mah MEH-zah pah-rah DOYSH, pohr fah-VOHR)

5. Can you recommend a good restaurant?: Pode recomendar um bom restaurante? (POH-deh reh-koh-mehn-DAHR oom BOHM reh-stow-RAHNG-tee?)

When attempting these expressions, keep in mind to speak slowly and clearly. Even though your pronunciation isn't great, the locals will nonetheless appreciate your attempts. A few simple words and phrases can go a long way toward improving the quality and success of your trip to Portugal.

GUIMARAES TRAVEL ITINERARIES

One-Day Explorations

Here are two one-day itineraries to help you make the most of your trip to Guimaraes if you only have a short amount of time there.

Alternative 1: The historic Guimaraes

Morning:

- Visit the Guimaraes Castle, the cradle of Portugal, to begin your day. View the expansive views of the city from the castle's walls while exploring the castle's grounds.

- Visit the Dukes of Braganza's Palace, which is close by. This exquisitely preserved mediaeval palace provides a window into the area's illustrious past.

- Lunch: 3. Visit a neighbourhood eatery for a classic Portuguese lunch in the historic district. Consider trying some local fare like "Bacalhau" (salted codfish) or "Francesinha" (a filling sandwich).

- Visit the Nossa Senhora da Oliveira Church in the afternoon, a work of art built right in the middle of the city. Admire the beautiful interiors and its detailed façade.

  Explore the tiny stores, cafes, and old structures as you stroll through the lovely streets of the historic district.

- Evening: 6. Conclude your day with a stroll along the Tamega River's riverbanks while taking in the tranquil atmosphere.

Option 2: Try the wine at a Douro Valley vineyard.

Morning:

- Travel to the picturesque Douro Valley, an area famed for its vineyards and wines, by taking an early-morning train or by renting a car.

- When you arrive at a vineyard, you can begin the day with a guided walk of the terraced vineyards where you can discover more about the region's history and the winemaking process.

- Lunch: 3. Savour the tastes of traditional Portuguese food while sipping on local wines during a delicious lunch at a nearby winery.

- Afternoon: 4. Take part in a wine-tasting session and sample several Douro Valley wine kinds. Learn from the staff's expertise on the qualities and subtleties of each wine.

- Enjoy a leisurely boat ride along the Douro River while taking in the stunning scenery and slopes covered in vineyards.

- Evening: 6. Reminisce about the tastes and experiences of the Douro Valley as you return to Guimaraes and have a leisurely meal at a neighbourhood restaurant to cap off your day.

Remember that all alternatives are jam-packed with things to do, so you might need to change your itinerary depending on your pace and preferences. Whichever route you take, a day in Guimaraes will leave you with lifelong memories of this historic treasure of Portugal and its breathtaking surroundings.

Weekend Getaways

There are many wonderful weekend getaway possibilities within a few hours of Guimaraes if you have a spare weekend and wish to travel somewhere. Here are three great weekend getaway locations close to Guimaraes:

1. The Charming City of Bridges: Porto

- Why Go: Porto is a lively and beautiful city renowned for its breathtaking waterfront, beautiful old buildings, and delectable port wine.

    Visit the famous Dom Luis I Bridge, stroll through the winding alleyways of the Ribeira neighbourhood, and take a leisurely boat ride along the Douro River. Don't pass up the chance to sample some of Portugal's best wines and tour the renowned port wine vaults. The vibrant energy, lovely cafes, and vibrant cultural environment of Porto make it the perfect weekend vacation location.

Approximately 45 minutes by vehicle or 1 hour by rail are required for the trip from Guimaraes.

2. **Braga, Portugal's centre of religion**

- Why Go: As was previously said, Braga is regarded as the "Rome of Portugal" because of its extensive ecclesiastical history. To fully immerse yourself in the city's spiritual past, visit the Sé Cathedral, Bom Jesus do Monte Sanctuary, and the So Martinho de Dume ruins.

    For those interested in history and culture, Braga is a fascinating trip because of its lively atmosphere, bustling squares, and abundance of churches and chapels.

Travel time from Guimaraes: 20 minutes by train or about 30 minutes by automobile.

3. **Wine and Natural Beauty in the Douro Valley**

- Why Go: The Douro Valley is a UNESCO World Heritage Site known for its terraced vineyards and delectable wines, as was previously mentioned.

  Take in the gorgeous scenery while spending the weekend touring the vineyards and local wineries. The Douro Valley is a pleasant getaway from the city, whether you enjoy wine tastings, picturesque boat tours, or just unwinding in the great outdoors.

1.5 to 2 hours is the approximate driving time from Guimaraes.

- Make the most of your weekend break by planning your itinerary and thinking about arranging lodging and tours well in advance, especially during the busiest travel times. Check the opening times of restaurants and attractions as well to guarantee a smooth and comfortable journey.

Regardless of where you decide to go, these weekend excursions from Guimaraes will give you a taste of Portugal's varied landscapes, history, and culture, making your vacation an unforgettable one.

Extended Stay Adventures

You might take advantage of a longer stay in Guimaraes or the surrounding area to discover even more of Portugal's numerous attractions. Here are some fun long-term excursions to think about:

1. **A trip on the Douro River**

    - Set out on a multi-day trip along the Douro River to slowly explore the beautiful Douro Valley. Enjoy the gorgeous scenery, terraced vineyards, and quaint riverside villages.

        To fully experience Portugal's wine country, several cruise packages include excursions to nearby wineries and cultural attractions.

2. **Road trip across Porto and northern Portugal:**

- Take a road trip through northern Portugal by renting a car. Visit the attractive towns and cities in the area, including Porto, Braga, and Viana do Castelo.

  Enjoy the local cuisine, historical sites, and seaside landscape while travelling. You can take your time on this road trip and explore further into northern Portugal's cultural gems.

3. **Coastal investigation**

- Keep visiting to experience Portugal's breathtaking coastline. Visit some of the beaches in the Costa Verde area, like Vila do Conde, Póvoa de Varzim, and Esposende. Travel south to the Costa Nova, which is renowned for its vibrantly striped buildings and stunning sandy beaches, for a more relaxed coastal experience.

4. **Adventures in National Parks:**

- For those who enjoy being outside, Portugal's national parks provide an opportunity to commune with nature. Visit Peneda-Geres National Park, the only national park in Portugal, to go hiking, observe wildlife, and take in the beautiful mountain scenery.

5. **The South and Lisbon:**

- Visit Lisbon, the capital of Portugal, and take a tour through the south of the nation. Experience Lisbon's bustling cultural scene, revel in its gastronomic treats and explore its historic neighbourhoods. Travel to the Algarve region from Lisbon for some beach leisure and charming coastal towns.

6. The Santiago Way

- Embark on a journey along the well-known Camino de Santiago. Start your Camino Portugues tour in Porto, then follow the picturesque routes through the countryside and historic towns to Santiago de Compostela, Spain.

7. Cultural and linguistic immersion:

- To further your cultural immersion, think about signing up for a Portuguese language course. Learning the language will help you develop stronger relationships with people and have a more comprehensive understanding of Portuguese culture.

- **Advice**: Make sure your visa and travel paperwork are current and meet the requirements for your length of stay before starting any long-stay excursion. Study regional traditions, climatic conditions, and activities as well to get the most out of your extended study of Portugal.

A longer visit to Guimaraes and Portugal provides the chance to learn more about the nation's rich past, varied landscapes, and friendly hospitality while making lifelong memories.

CONCLUSION

Final Thoughts

It has been my pleasure to serve as your virtual tour guide as you explore Guimaraes and Portugal, as well as to inform you about numerous travel, cultural, and adventurous topics.

Any traveller will have a wonderful time in Portugal because of its colourful history, stunning scenery, and dynamic culture.

1. Don't forget to explore the city's famous sites, such as the Guimaraes Castle and the Palace of the Dukes of Braganza, to fully immerse yourself in its fascinating past. Enjoy the regional food and the friendliness of the Portuguese people as you stroll through the quaint streets of the old centre.

2. Beyond Guimaraes, you might travel to Porto for its entrancing riverbank environment, Braga for its ecclesiastical legacy, or the Douro Valley for a wine-sampling excursion.

3. Take advantage of the chance to learn some fundamental Portuguese words and phrases when you travel because it will improve your relationships with locals and show that you value their culture.

4. Remember to travel wisely, keep aware of safety and health issues, and be open to embracing new experiences and relationships as you continue your journey, whether it be a quick weekend break or an extended stay adventure.

I hope you have a wonderful time in Guimaraes and Portugal and discover new things about the country's culture. Greetings and safe travels! Please feel free to come back whenever you need more help or have more questions. Happy adventuring!

Printed in Great Britain
by Amazon